C000120579

Basenji
20 Milestone Challenges

Basenji Memorable Moments. Includes Milestones for Memories, Gifts, Socialization & Training

Volume 1

Todays Doggy

Copyright © 2019

Dedicated To All of You Wonderful Owners and Fans

Introduction

Welcome to the Original Doggy Milestone Series™ where you are encouraged to create those special moments with your dog. We have composed the milestones in a way that challenges you to set the stage before taking your photos.

Use props and make it fun - be creative in setting up your photos. Get family and friends involved - take it out with you - use it in different places and settings - have a play with it and most importantly, have a good time!

You can either hold the desired milestone spread open yourself - or have somebody hold it open as you take the snap.

If you would like to have the selected milestone book spread open and standing independently in your photos, you can use one or two large 'foldback' clips to hold the spread open.

Good luck and enjoy your photo fun.

I Love My Family...

...And My Family Loves Me

At The
Beach!

Having
a
Wave
of a
Time

With My Doggy Pals

IT'S...

BED
TIME

I DIDN'T KNOW WHICH STICK YOU THREW

SO I BOUGHT BACK ALL OF THEM

They Say
Diamonds
Are a Girl's
Best Friend

I Disagree! I'm The Only "Best Friend" Here!

I'm Going To Start Eating Healthy...

Next
Week!

DO
NOT
DISTURB

PLAYING

IN THE

LEAVES

I Need a **HUG**e

Amount
Of
Treats

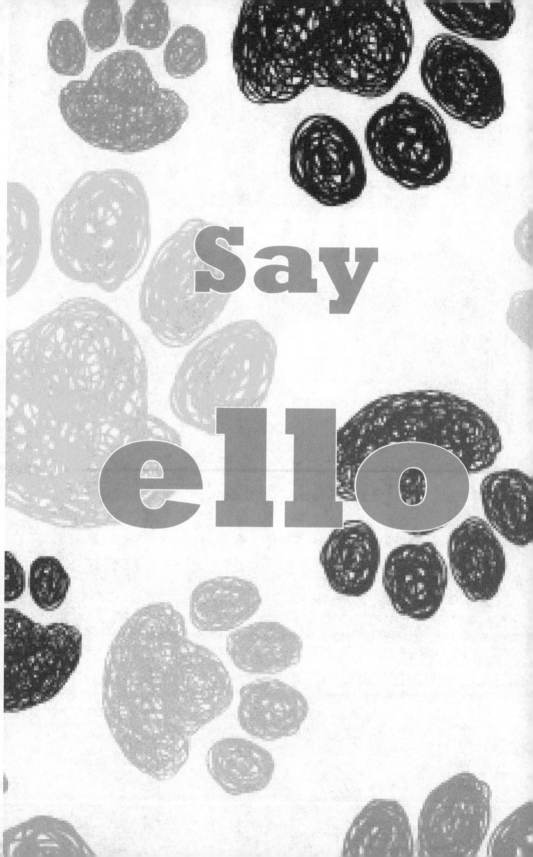

To My Little Friend

OFF
To
The
VET??

CATCH ME IF YOU CAN!

KEEP CALM

WE'RE A TEAM

NASA

Wants

To Hire

Me

Because

I'm a

STAR!

OOPS!
I
Buried
Your
Stuff

...But I Forgot Where

I'm a

Super

Hero

My
Real
Name
Is
SUPER
POOCH

Very
Incredible
Pup

I
DIDN'T
DO IT

I'll Just Be Be Over Here...

Looking

Fabulous

PLEASE

PLEASE

PRETTY PLEEEEASE

CAN I KEEP IT?

I'm On a SEAFOOD Diet

CPSIA information can be obtained
at www.ICGtesting.com
Printed in the USA
LVHW080403210819
628320LV00007B/227/P